I0481823

Temporary Residence Application:
For Canadian Immigration

Temporary Residence Application

For Canadian Immigration

Charles Mwewa

Kitchener, Canada
2018

First Printing: 2018

ISBN-13: 978-1722436230
ISBN-10: 1722436239

Charles Mwewa
16 Manitou Drive
Suite 16
Kitchener, ON N2C 2J6
Canada

Dedication

For Clarice, with Love!

Contents

Introduction

Canadian immigration and refugee process is divided into three sets: Temporary Residence; Permanent Residence; and Citizenship. This booklet explores Temporary Residence and the questions that immigration and refugee officers have to consider to determine whether the person's claimed reason/s for temporary immigration are, in fact, the assumed reasons. Canadian Permanent Residents and Canadian Citizens have full rights accorded to them by law. Temporary residents are just so, temporary. Therefore, to be granted a VISA – whether as a student, visitor, tourist, accompanying parent or temporary worker – one has to satisfy an immigration officer that they intend to leave Canada at the end of their stay, among other requirements.

Chapter 1
VISAs Overview

❝A foreign national may not enter Canada to remain on a temporary basis without first obtaining a temporary resident visa" (Regulations, *infra*, s. 7(1)).

A Temporary Resident Visa (TRV) is an official counterfoil document issued by a visa office that is placed in a person's passport to show that they have met the requirements for admission to Canada as a temporary resident. Holding a TRV does not guarantee entry to Canada. The admission of foreign nationals into Canada as temporary residents is a privilege, not a right.

To be given a TRV, various factors will be considered, and these will include the purpose of the trip, the duration of the trip, ties to Canada, and other factors. Other factors are very critical to the application process but they do not in themselves impact negatively upon the application process. These "other" factors are valid travel documents (such as a passport or travel document), how the applicant will support themselves in Canada, whether they have a criminal record or a serious illness.

Generally, some people are not allowed to come to Canada. They are known as "inadmissible" under Canada's immigration law. There are many reasons Canada may not let some applicants into Canada, such as: They are a security risk; they have committed human or international rights violations; they have been convicted of a crime, or they have committed an act outside Canada that would be a crime in Canada; they have ties to organized crime; they have a serious health problem; they have a serious financial problem; they have lied in their application or in an interview before; they do not meet the conditions in Canada's immigration law; or one of their family members is not allowed into Canada. Normally, if an applicant is inadmissible to Canada, they will not be allowed to enter. If they have a valid reason to travel to Canada, Canada may issue them a **Temporary Resident Permit** (TRP).

As of July 31st, 2018, applicants will need to give their fingerprints and photos (biometrics) when they apply for a visitor visa, study or work permit, or permanent residence if they are from Europe, the Middle East or Africa. If the applicant has provided biometric information before, the Visa Office may already have the results of the biometric checks. Biometric results help immigration officers know more about the applicant – whether they are not inadmissible or whether they are a person who may require authorization to return to Canada, and so on. As of July 31st, 2018, all those who apply for temporary resident visas will be required to provide biometrics. If an applicant has had their application for temporary resident visa refused, officers may have their biometrics already.

HINT 1: "A person who makes an application must answer truthfully all questions put to them for the purpose of the examination and must produce a visa and all relevant evidence and documents that the officer reasonably requires."

The author of this little booklet assumes two things: First, that the applicant is not inadmissible to Canada. If the applicant is found to be inadmissible to Canada, the suggestions offered in this booklet will be irrelevant. To not be inadmissible is a presumption under Canadian immigration law. In other words, an applicant is presumed to be not inadmissible unless proved otherwise.

Second, that the applicant will "answer truthfully all questions put to them for the purpose of the examination and must produce a visa and all relevant evidence and documents that the officer reasonably requires." This is definitive; there is no room for error. If the applicant does not answer truthfully, the **hints** provided in this booklet will be immaterial.

The letter of invitation should be sent to the person being invited to Canada, who will include it with the TRV application, and must contain the following information about:[1]

The person being invited	The person inviting the foreign national
<ul><li>complete name;</li><li>date of birth;</li><li>the address and telephone number;</li></ul>	<ul><li>complete name;</li><li>date of birth;</li><li>address and telephone number in Canada;</li><li>occupation;</li></ul>

---

[1] IRCC, "Letter of Invitation," available online at https://www.canada.ca/en/immigration-refugees-citizenship/corporate/publications-manuals/operational-bulletins-manuals/temporary-residents/visitors/evidence-supporting-purpose-entry.html (retrieved: July 1st, 2018)

The person being invited	The person inviting the foreign national
<ul><li>the relationship with the person being invited;</li><li>the purpose of the trip;</li><li>length of intended stay in Canada;</li><li>details on accommodation and living expenses; and</li><li>the intended</li></ul>	<ul><li>whether they are a Canadian citizen or permanent resident; and</li><li>a photocopy of a document proving their status in Canada</li></ul>

The person being invited	The person inviting the foreign national
date of departure from Canada.	

Three Types of TRVs

Transit Visa: This is needed to travel through Canada without stopping or visiting. This visa is required even if the applicant will be in Canada for less than 48 hours. There is no fee for a transit visa.

Single-Entry Visa: It allows the temporary foreign national to enter Canada only once during the visa's period of validity. It may be issued up to six months before the expected date of travel. And it should have an expiry date of at least one month after the expected date of arrival in Canada.

Multiple-Entry Visa: It allows the holder to seek entry into Canada from any country as often as necessary during the visa's period of validity. It is issued with long-term validity to facilitate entry into Canada for legitimate travellers. It has a maximum validity date of up to ten years or one month before the expiry date on the travel document. It should now be considered the standard document to issue, and any single-entry visa issuance requires officers to provide an explanation recorded in the application. It can still be valid but affixed in an expired travel document.[2]

---

[2] In that case, the holder must also be in possession of a newer and valid travel document and must present both travel documents to the airline carrier in order to travel to Canada and to the border services officer in order to seek entry into Canada.

Four Categories of TRVs

Super Visas: Pursuant to subsection 15(4) of the Act, which authorizes the officer to conduct the examination in accordance with any instructions that the Minister may give, the Super visa concerns the parents and grandparents who wish to extend their temporary resident visa for authorized period of extended stay. It is a multiple-entry TRV for up to 10 years, with the status period extending for up to two years on each entry to Canada.

Diplomatic and Official Visas: It is evidence of Canada's *consent* to official visits by foreign officials under International Law. It is consent granted to diplomatic, consular or official (functional) privileges and immunities (or courtesies).[3]

Courtesy Visas: This category of TRVs may be granted on courtesy to persons who

---

[3] This booklet will not discuss in any more details about diplomatic or official visas; this booklet is meant for common temporary travellers only.

are not entitled to diplomatic privileges and immunities but who are, by virtue of their position or reason for coming to Canada, considered of sufficient importance to warrant a visa to facilitate their admission.

Facilitation Visas: Immigration, Refugee and Citizenship Canada (IRCC) can sometimes "facilitate" the travel of a dual national by placing a facilitation visa counterfoil into the passport of the Canadian's other nationality. It is done, usually, where not facilitating their travel would result in undue hardship. It is not a pretext for "hiding" from governments that do not permit dual citizenship.

Types of Applicants

This booklet covers students, visitors, tourists and temporary workers. There are other types of applicants that may be of interest to immigration offers. These may include:

Minors:[4] Minors travelling alone require a letter from both parents authorizing
them to travel. Minors travelling with one
parent require a letter of authorization from
the non-accompanying parent. When travelling alone, minors must be in possession of
a passport or travel document issued in their
own name. They cannot travel with the passport or travel document of a parent (on
which they are listed) unless the holder of
the document (parent) accompanies them.
Persons seeking entry at the POE with a
child will be asked to produce the above-
mentioned documentation. If they are not in
possession of such documents, they may be
required to provide the telephone numbers
for the child's parent(s) and/or other documentation to satisfy an officer of the child's
safety and well-being. It is the mandate of
IRCC, in conjunction with the federal *Our*

---

[4] These guidelines are reproduced from, IRCC,
"Temporary residents: Requirements for minors," available
online at https://www.canada.ca/en/immigration-refugees-
citizenship/corporate/publications-manuals/operational-
bulletins-manuals/temporary-residents/visitors/require-
ments-minors.html (July 1st, 2018)

Missing Children Program,[5] to ensure that the child is in the custody of an approved parent or guardian.

If a guardian is travelling with the minor, the guardian should present a statement from the parent(s), which: authorizes the child to travel with someone else; provides the name and telephone of the guardian; and indicates the destination and the period of time the child will be in Canada. The child should have original identity documents.[6] If the minor is the subject of a custody order or is in a single-parent family, a copy of the custody order is required; or proof of custody and/or the other parent's written consent for the trip.

---

[5] See http://www.rcmp-grc.gc.ca/omc-ned/index-accueil-eng.htm

[6] If the officer is not satisfied with the letter's authenticity, a faxed version of a parent's consent letter would be acceptable. The final decision rests with the POE officer. If minor children entering as students have the proper identity documents, they should not have any problems entering Canada.

Charles Mwewa

Business Persons and Business Delegations:[7] Officers should determine whether or not the business visitor has the ability to undertake the business proposed in Canada. Checking with the visa office's trade section to obtain its opinion as to the legitimacy of the companies is one method of verifying the visitor's background. Organizers of the delegation and supporting companies may be asked to provide documentation in support of the visit. Random interviews with individuals may be necessary to ensure that the delegation is genuine. It may be necessary to assess the *bona fides* of the inviting enterprise in Canada, as some invitations may be made specifically to facilitate the entry of non-legitimate visitors to Canada. Any visa office dealing with business travellers originating outside its area of jurisdiction should carefully scrutinize all documentation and,

---

[7] These guidelines are reproduced from, IRCC, "Temporary residents: Business persons and business delegations," available online at https://www.canada.ca/en/immigration-refugees-citizenship/corporate/publications-manuals/operational-bulletins-manuals/temporary-residents/visitors/business-persons-business-delegations.html (retrieved: July 1st, 2018)

where *bona fides* are questionable, request assistance from the visa office responsible for the applicant's normal place of residence.

Persons Wishing to Enter Canada for the Purpose of Giving Birth:[8] Under paragraph 3(1)(a) of the *Citizenship Act*,[9] persons born in Canada are Canadian citizens. This right applies to all persons born in Canada, irrespective of the status in Canada of their parents, other than persons born to accredited diplomats. There are no elements of the [Act] which refer to this right. Giving birth in Canada does not represent a violation of any terms or conditions which may be applied to a temporary resident. Thus, there is no provision in the [Act] to refuse a

---

[8] These guidelines are reproduced from, IRCC, "Temporary residents: Persons wishing to enter Canada for the purpose of giving birth," available online at https://www.canada.ca/en/immigration-refugees-citizenship/corporate/publications-manuals/operational-bulletins-manuals/temporary-residents/visitors/persons-wishing-enter-canada-purpose-giving-birth.html ((retrieved: July 1st, 2018)

[9] R.S.C., 1985, c. C-29

TRV solely on the basis of the intent of the applicant to give birth in Canada.

When it is known that an applicant is pregnant, assessment of the application should focus on the requirements applied to all applicants for a TRV. The fact of the pregnancy may be an element in the assessment but only in so far as it affects the assessment of the primary requirements for issuance of a TRV:

- Do applicants have sufficient funds?
- Will they leave Canada at the end of their period of authorized stay?
- Are they admissible?

Consideration of the pregnancy and the stated or apparent intent to give birth in Canada must relate back to one of these essential requirements for TRV issuance. Guidelines for persons coming forward for medical treatment may provide officers with assistance in assessing applications from persons who are known to be pregnant and intending to give birth in Canada at the time of the TRV application. However, it is important to note that pregnancy would not normally present concerns regarding medical inadmissibility.

While a "high-risk" pregnancy might create excessive demands, this would normally be speculative and would not apply to the future child, who would become a citizen at birth; concerns regarding the demands that may be placed on health and social services by the child after birth in Canada may not be used in assessing the medical admissibility of the TRV applicant.

In applying the guidelines on temporary residents seeking medical treatment in Canada, officers should focus on available financial support as part of their assessment of admissibility. A medical examination should only be requested in exceptional cases, where the information from the examination would be material to the assessment of the application. The application form for a TRV asks the applicant if they or any accompanying family members have any physical or mental disorders that will require social or health services during their stay in Canada. Answering "No" to this question should not normally be considered misrepresentation in the case of pregnant applicants, given the terminology used. Pregnancy may not normally be viewed as a "medical condition." However, pregnancy or the intent to give birth in Canada may be material facts in the assessment of the application which, if we are not advised of the pregnancy, may go unexamined; such facts may be material to the assessment of arrangements for treatment, of the financial ability to cover the costs of treatment, or of the intent to depart from Canada, for example. Therefore, in some cases the intentional concealment of intent to give birth in Canada may lead to an examination of admissibility under section 40 of the Act.

Intending Organ Donors:[10] The following procedures apply when assessing a

---

[10] For more information, see IRCC, "Temporary resident applications from intending organ donors," available online at https://www.canada.ca/en/immigration-refugees-citizenship/corporate/publications-manuals/operational-bulletins-manuals/temporary-residents/visitors/applications-intending-organ-donors.html (retrieved: July 1st, 2018)

Temporary Residence Application

TRV application from an applicant wishing to enter Canada for the purpose of donating an organ to a Canadian citizen or permanent resident in Canada. Three criteria should guide the initial assessment of the application: (1) Evidence of medical compatibility between the donor and the recipient; (2) Evidence of satisfactory financial arrangements; and (3) Evidence that a sale of human organ is not being transacted.

Chapter 2
Purpose of the Trip

The purpose of the trip must be temporary in nature. It must not be a ploy or a route to permanent residence or citizenship. An immigration officer must be satisfied that the applicant's sole reason and motive to apply for a TRV is temporary residence. If there is any inclination or reason to believe that the reason is other than temporary residence, the application will be denied. Sometimes applicants assert and state that they want to immigrate temporarily when they have intentions to remain in Canada illegally, to claim refugee status or seek to remain in Canada for other reasons other than temporary residence.

All temporary foreign nationals seeking entry to Canada must be able to satisfy an officer at the POE or an officer at Case Processing Centre (CPC) that they have a genuine purpose for wishing to come into or remain in Canada. According to Canadian immigration guidelines, this can be accomplished by providing:

- An invitation letter (which can be verified) from the family/friends/colleagues to be visited in Canada, outlining the reason and length of the visit;
- Contact numbers for persons who may be able to substantiate the stated purpose for coming or remaining in Canada; and
- Any other documentation that may substantiate the purpose.

HINT 2: Do not indicate anywhere or supply evidence or information that will show that you will not abide by the requirement to leave Canada at the end of the period authorized for the temporary stay!

Dual intent (two intentions) or multiple intentions (more than two intentions) to remain in Canada is not proscribed under the

Immigration and Refugee Protection Act[11] (the "Act") and the Immigration and Refugee Protection Regulations[12] (the "Regulations"). Many people who are fleeing from persecution, for example, may be denied a TRV if the officer knows that refugee claiming is the eventual intent for the trip. However, the officers know or ought to know that for refugee claimants, giving the right reason for the trip may be liability or even put the applicant's life in greater danger than stating the true intentions. Habit and common-sense has informed that, where an applicant has dual or multiple intent for applying for temporary residence, the only reason that counts during the application process is the temporary reason. Other reasons may be revealed later either at the POE (airport or border or sea coast) or inland (inside Canada). Dual intent is permitted under Canadian immigration law, but only when it is connected to permanent residence. Having two intents – one for temporary residence

---

[11] S.C. 2001, c. 27
[12] SOR/2002-227

and one for permanent residence – is legitimate:

"An intention by a foreign national to become a permanent resident does not preclude them from becoming a temporary resident if the officer is satisfied that they will leave Canada by the end of the period authorized for their stay."[13]

Dual intent is present when a foreign national who has applied for permanent residence in Canada also applies to enter Canada for a temporary period as a visitor, worker or student. Dual intent on the part of the applicant is, therefore, not *prima facie* ground for refusal of temporary resident status.[14] In other words, when an applicant has first applied for permanent residence, they

---

[13] Act, s.22(2)
[14] IRCC, "Temporary residents: Dual intent applicants" available online at
https://www.canada.ca/en/immigration-refugees-citizenship/corporate/publications-manuals/operational-bulletins-manuals/temporary-residents/visitors/dual-intent-applicants.html (retrieved: July 1st, 2018)

can also apply for temporary residence under the doctrine of dual intent.

HINT 3: An applicant may have eventual intent to become a permanent resident, but in order to qualify for a temporary resident visa, they must demonstrate that (1) they will return to their country of residence or citizenship, or (2) they have the capacity and willingness to leave Canada at the end of the authorized temporary period.

Chapter 3
Duration of the Trip

The purpose and duration of the trip are related. A tourist and a student may not claim the same number of days to remain in Canada, for example. A tourist may require fewer days than a student. The same is true for a temporary worker and a student.

HINT 4: The purpose of your trip will inform the duration of the trip. Suggest as fewer days as possible to remain in Canada and leave the final duration to the discretion of the officer.

The duration and purpose of the trip are tied to what the applicant will be doing in Canada. Doing nothing is not a reason and such applications will likely be denied. The frequent mistake made by many applicants is to assume that because the applicant has a letter of acceptance, for example, that the purpose of the trip is studying. That may be the reason stated on the acceptance letter. But the real reason must be stated in the application. The eventual reason for the trip is what the applicant's **plans** are for visiting Canada. A well-executed plan will clear this hurdle. Rather than just state "study" as the reason, the applicant must elaborate in some details how they intent to fulfil that purpose. The plan must be well thought out; it must not be vexatious, frivolous or flippant. What the officer wants to know is the real motivation for the trip, not just want is stated. All applicants who wish to visit Canada should have detailed plans or a recognized idea of what they will be doing in Canada

---

HINT 5: Request for a limited duration (duration with start date and end date) and not an indeterminate duration.

Your indicated purpose of the trip and the requested duration will be considered in the context of the applicant's home country. For example, is it reasonable for an applicant coming from a country where war has just been declared or where civil war has been going on for a long time to request to remain in Canada for only seven days or not to have eventual intentions to claim for refugee status? In this situation a longer period may be reasonable. However, a tourist who indicates intention to see the CN Tower in Toronto and the Niagara Falls in Niagara may be denied a VISA if she requests more time than necessary to remain in Canada.

HINT 6: The duration of time requested must be reasonable, plausible and practical.

Chapter 4
Ties to Canada or Country of Residence

Ties to your country of residence and your stated reason for the trip are related. They may expose your motive. The officer will ask: Are ties to the applicant's home country sufficiently strong to ensure that the applicant is motivated to return home after the visit to Canada?

A classic example is that of an applicant who is a temporary or permanent residence of another country and who is applying for temporary residence in Canada. For such an applicant, the ties to their home country are too weak to satisfy an officer that they will leave Canada and return to their country of residence or citizenship at the end of their stay. This thinking is pure commonsense, but could be supported by facts and the law, too.

Generally, an applicant who is not employed in their country of residence or citizenship; or who does not own any property in their country of residence or citizenship, may not convince the officer that they will return to their home country. For those who are employed, their level of salary, position at work and whether or not the employer has approved a request for leave, also matter. If the salary is below that of economic comfort, it could be presumed, or even assumed, that they are seeking immigrating to Canada to seek a better life permanently. If the applicant has a low position at work, it may be construed as looking for an exit, or if the employer has not granted permission for leave, the applicant may not be intending to return to their home country. While there are refugee and immigration programs that guarantee this aspect of purpose, temporary residence is not one of them. Under temporary residence, the applicant must satisfy the officer that they will return to their home country. The level of establishment in their home country will determine whether they are granted the TRV.

HINT 7: A good job with an attractive salary within a thriving company and holding a good position in the company, in addition to the employer granting an applicant leave, may go a long way to satisfying the officer of strong ties to the applicant's home country.

Moreover, the following issues may be considered by the officer:

- Does the applicant have property?
- What is the value of the property?
- What financial obligation is the person leaving behind?
- What is the nature and value of these obligations?
- What other responsibilities and obligations is the applicant leaving behind?
- How will they be discharged?
- Is travel consistent with local customs or practices?
- Has the applicant travelled before?

The **Travel History Report** (or the prior history of the applicant's travels) may be considered. It is a record of a traveller's entries into Canada. The pages of the applicant's passport are, by default, the record of all travels. Some countries may require a record of travels while for others, the passport is adequate. The history of one's travels can be an asset or liability depending on whether it is the first trip, whether previous conditions have been violated, or whether the trip is necessary in the context of other competing factors which may be economic or political. Even if the person's ties to the home country seem to be strong, there may be other factors in the general economic or political environment which might make the long-term prospects for the applicant or their family unstable. The officer has discretion to consider all these "other" factors.

> **HINT 8:** The weaker the ties to the applicant's home country, the less likely the applicant will be granted a TRV.

Another consideration is the applicant's ties to Canada. These ties should be strong enough to compensate for weaker ties to the applicant's home country. Where an applicant has strong ties to their home country, weaker ties to Canada may be compensated by stronger ties to their home country. The applicant whose ties to her home country is weak and ties to Canada are equally weak, is unlikely to be granted a TRV.

In answering what ties an applicant has in Canada, a few things ought to be reviewed: The person or institution that invites the applicant to Canada. Canada's immigration law recognizes the value and importance of relationships. Strong and enduring relationships are rewarded while weaker or frivolous ones are shunned. Certain relationships may not even meet the requirements of the Act and Regulations. As a rule, family relationships are honoured in Canadian law – as one of the chief objectives of Immigration and Refugee law is family reunification.

The inviting entity is as important as the evidence of the inviting host. Principally, an applicant who has a family or relatives who are Canadian permanent residents or citizens are preferable. Those who are invited by mere acquaintances or institutions may not have the same level of leverage. And this is important for security and national security interest reasons.

HINT 9: Who is inviting; proof of an invitation letter; and the immigration status in Canada of the inviting entity are important.

The applicant's family ties to her home country is as important as her family ties to Canada. The type of family the applicant has in the country of residence is a vital factor. A strong united family with at least the minimum of a nucleus family standard is preferred. This is because it guarantees more safety and stability and may convince the officer that the applicant will return to it. A disintegrated and dysfunctional family arrangement or where the applicant lacks such strong family ties to her home country, may lead to the rejection of the TRV application. Important, too, is the state of the family unit of the applicant at the time of application. It does not count if the family was once united and together; if at the time of application there is question as to the stability of the family in the home country, the application may be rejected.

Chapter 5
Proof of Support

There is no constitutional requirement for Canada to support financially temporary foreign nationals. Temporary residents do not have a *right* to be supported financially or economically by any level of the Canadian government. Only permanent residents and citizens have that right. As part of the application process, a temporary resident must, therefore, provide proof of how they will support themselves in Canada. This is evidentiary based. In other words, a temporary resident applicant should show proof of funds or assets of how they will provide for themselves in Canada.

The gregarious and magnanimous nature of the Canadian immigration policy guarantees that applicants should show how they will provide for themselves in Canada in two ways: Either personally or through someone else who will provide for them. In the first place, the applicant should have the means to be self-supporting or someone else must be *willing* and *able* to provide adequate support. This will largely depend on other factors, such as whether the applicant will be staying in hotels or with relatives or friends. Whether the applicant will be travelling within Canada, and if so, for how long and how often.

In the second place, the applicant must indicate what is her source of funds: Are they traveller's cheques or credit cards? Or is it cash – and if so, will it be declared at customs? Or is it other sources of funds – and the applicant will be required to indicate what this source or sources are or will be. Certain countries also may have currency re-strictions. The applicant must take this into account if she is applying from such a home country.

HINT 10: Link amount and source of funds to the purpose and duration of stay. If longer stay, applicant must show evidence of adequate funds to last for the duration requested for. The secret is not for the applicant or the person or entity supporting them to later be a financial burden on the Canadian government.

The danger of not having adequate or enough funds for the temporary foreign national is that it can lead to illegal activities. Temporary foreign nationals must have enough funds to maintain themselves in Canada without resorting to illegal employment or social assistance.

Some TRVs allow temporary foreign nationals to work in Canada. If the applicant intends to work or study in Canada, they should have a valid work or study permit. Most temporary foreign nationals who work or study in Canada must have their work or study permit approved before arriving in Canada. Some Student Visas allow for work within the named institution up to 20 hours per week. Despite this condition, applicants should understand that working may be incidental to studying. The requirement to satisfy the officer still remains that the applicant has enough funds to sustain the purpose of the trip to Canada.

Chapter 6
Ability to Leave Canada

The applicant must be able to leave Canada at the end of their stated reason or purpose of the trip. The ability to leave Canada is evidentiary based. In short, it is not a mere declaration. The applicant must show the evidence that they will return to their home country. This is, usually, demonstrated by having the financial ability to return and a valid passport or travel document.

Having the financial ability to return to the home country is demonstrated by showing that the applicant has already bought an airplane ticket. The applicant can also demonstrate the ability to leave Canada by showing that they have enough money or a statement of bank assets.

The other way of demonstrating the ability to return is through a valid and subsisting passport, travel document and/or visa which will admit the person to the home country or to a third country. The expiry date on the passport or travel document must be "valid for the period authorized for their stay."[15]

> # Hint 11: To be valid and sub-
> sisting, make sure that the passport or travel document will *allow* the applicant re-entry to the country which issued the document.

---

[15] Regulations, s. 52